New York

THIS IS A CARLTON BOOK

This edition published by Carlton Publishing Group 2002
20 Mortimer Street
London
W1T 3JW

A CIP catalogue for this book is available from the British Library.

ISBN 1 84222 701 7

Executive Editor: Sarah Larter
Design: Adam Wright/Simon Mercer
Picture research: Claire Gouldstone
Production: Janette Burgin

Printed in Dubai

New York

WILL JONES

CARLTON BOOKS

AS SEEN
ON
SAMSUNG
SAMSUNG
SUNTORY
WHISKY
Enjoy
Coke
MARQUIS
VISA
novotel

LG
LG
semiconduc
Come Eat With Us!
NEW YORK
CRITERION CENTER
Roundabout Theatre
Stage Right
Laura Pels Theatre
The Rehearsal
Grace & Glorie
XANADU
CRITERION CE
Roundabout Theatre Company
Get tested.

In a few fatal minutes on the morning of September 11, 2001, America was struck at its very core when two airplanes flew into the World Trade Center. Long after the last wreath has been laid and the final remnants of the destruction taken away, the city will ponder the long-term effects of the murderous destruction of thousands of lives and of two of the most easily identifiable buildings on the planet.

The terrorist attack on the World Trade Centers also sent shock waves racing through the architectural community. The virtually simultaneous destruction of these iconic twins dealt a massive blow to the aspirations of a generation of architects who had worked in the knowledge that, while in other parts of the world limits and constraints held them back, in the United States almost anything was possible. The skyscraper, defining architecture of capitalism, the USA and New York, was now reclassified as terrorist target.

Tall buildings are synonymous with the US, particularly New York. Until 1996, when the Petronas Towers were built in Malaysia, no other country had ever been able to lay claim to having the tallest building in the world. Designed, ironically, by US architect Cesar Pelli, the Petronas Towers rose from the bustle of Kuala Lumpur to a height of 450 metres. Until then the USA had reigned supreme. Chicago's Sears Tower stands at 443 metres, followed by the towers of the World Trade Center, which stood at 417 metres, and there are a host of other one-time "world's tallest" including the Empire State and Chrysler Buildings.

Before the race skywards began, New York was a city built in a neo-classical image, with architects taking reference from Roman and Greek forms. The tallest structure in New York in the 1880s was the Brooklyn Bridge. Twenty-four years in the making, the bridge spans a staggering 486 metres and its colossal stone towers stand 84 metres above the high water line. Tragically the bridge took the life of the engineer mastermind behind it. German-born John Augustus Roebling crushed his foot while on site, and, refusing any medication for his injury because "it would dull his brain", he died soon after from gangrene.

NEW YORK

Work continued, now overseen by his son Washington Roebling. He too was to suffer at the hands of the bridge, though. Pressurized techniques used to construct the foundations deep under the East River caused Roebling junior to be struck down with caisson disease, more commonly known as the bends. He was bedridden for the remainder of the bridge's construction and directed work from a nearby hotel room overlooking the site.

Although Americans pioneered skyscraper design, the origins of construction with metal and especially the iron and steel frame hark from across the Atlantic in the United Kingdom. In 1792 mill owner W. Strutt used vertical iron supports to carry timber beams in his mills in Derby and Belper. Soon after mills and factories were being built with the first iron frames or skeletons.

This innovation revolutionized construction techniques. No longer were thick heavy masonry walls needed to support the building, instead the façade was supported by a steel frame. However, it took a French engineer named Gustave Eiffel to exploit the true potential of the metal frame. He took it to quite literally new heights in 1889 with his famous Eiffel Tower. Built for the Paris Exhibition of that year, the tower reached an impressive 300 metres high. It became the tallest man-made structure in the world and would keep the title for 41 years, until New York's skyscraper race of the 1930s.

American architects and engineers embraced metal frame construction. They saw, through Eiffel's example, the potential of this new lightweight frame construction and set about creating buildings, the height of which had only previously been dreamed about.

As a new century dawned, New York was in the cast iron architectural revolution. The technique of casting multiple identical building sections in a factory, and then transporting them to site presaged modern curtain wall construction and the theory behind skyscraper design. Cast iron is lighter than masonry and its strength allows for larger apertures in building façades. Buildings could be higher and still be well lit inside.

In 1903 one of New York's finest examples of cast iron architecture was completed. Standing on a triangular site where Fifth Avenue and Broadway cross is the Fuller Building.

NEW YORK

Widely known as the Flatiron, due to its shape, it is one of New York's first steel frame skyscrapers. Designed by Daniel Burnham, the Flatiron's façade is draped in ornamentation – from the top down, there is a balustrade and cornice, a band of maidens peeping out from blocks between the windows, a row of two-storey round-headed windows and a large pride of lion heads, scowling down from on high. And this is all on the top third of the 21-storey, 93.5 metre-high Flatiron. Buildings were starting to get taller.

At around the same time steam trains were phased out in favour of electric rolling stock and work started on what would become the hub of New York's transport infrastructure, Grand Central Station. Completed in 1913, the station, which was designed by Warren & Wetmore, Reed & Stem Architects, is awe-inspiring. Underneath the busy city streets lie rail tracks spanning nearly fourteen city blocks, stretching from Lexington Avenue to Madison and from 42nd to 50th Streets. In all there are over one hundred platforms and in the 1940s over 600 trains used the station every day.

Above ground the station is hardly less impressive. Minnesota architects Reed & Stem won the station commission in 1903. Their team included Whitney Warren and Charles Wetmore who, after Reed died in 1911, took over the project. Whitney's Beaux-Arts education had a great influence on the design of the building. The wondrous barrel-vaulted ceiling in the main concourse rises to a height of 38 metres, giving the space the air of cathedral rather than station.

"I DO **NOT** WANT A mere building. I WANT SOMETHING THAT WILL BE AN **ORNAMENT** TO THE city."

Completed in the same year was the Woolworth building. While Grand Central eulogized the interior of a cathedral, the Woolworth building became known as the "cathedral of commerce" for its beautifully crafted exterior. Architect Cass Gilbert designed what would be the tallest building in the world for the next sixteen years, in a fifteenth century French Gothic style. The building is one of the first to incorporate a slim tower on a large base and is seen as a prelude to the 1915 ordinances to ensure set-back on all tall buildings so as not to lose light at pavement level.

The Woolworth Building was paid for in cash by Frank Winfield Woolworth, founder of the Woolworth brand. He recognized the potential of owning the world's tallest building and instructed Gilbert to build it to beat the record. Woolworth had a somewhat strained relationship with Gilbert, once stating, after revising the architect's drawings: "I do not want a mere building. I want something that will be an ornament to the city." The result is still breathtaking today.

1914 saw the start of the First World War. Although the US was not involved in the fighting until 1917, it was providing manufacturing and financial help to the United Kingdom. Each and every day Britain was spending $10 million, of which some $4 million was being raised in loans in the US markets. When the America entered the war on April 6, 1917 architecture had to take a back seat. The war was to cost the United States $25 billion and in the coming years the country would be slow to restart its building programme. In New York, as business recovered to normal levels of trading, the Art Deco style took hold and a new breed of skyscraper emerged.

In the three years between 1928 and 1931 New York was to witness the greatest ever architectural race for the skies. Initially, two rivals for the title of tallest building in New York and the world went head to head – the Chrysler Building at 405 Lexington and the Bank of Manhattan Building 40 Wall Street.

Designed by William van Alen, the Chrysler Building was and is a spectacular homage to the Art Deco movement. Its challenger, the now neglected Bank of Manhattan Building, was designed by Van Alen's ex-partner and arch-rival H. Craig Severance, in a more conventional style. Height was what mattered to Severance and when he found out that the Chrysler was going to be 282 metres tall he added a 15 metre flag pole, taking the Bank of Manhattan Building to 282.5 metres. But Van Alen had a secret weapon. In August 1930 he unveiled the "vertex", a spire made of chrome and nickel that was assembled in the chrome-clad dome of the Chrysler and raised from within, elevating the building's final height to 319.5 metres. The Chrysler Building's spire even surpassed the height of the Eiffel Tower, giving it the title of tallest man-made structure in the world.

For all the building's swagger at reaching new heights, it is the intricate art deco ornamentation that is its most wonderful feature. Both inside and out the Chrysler building exudes elegance. From the shimmering silver dome and spire to the eight giant eagle-headed gargoyles glaring down at passers by, the exterior is enchanting in its beauty. Inside, the stunning triangular lobby, shrouded in onyx, marble and granite sets the tone. The lifts, lined with an array of polished timbers, glide smoothly from the lobby to the Cloud Club in the building's dome. This became a haven for New York's millionaires during the prohibition years; members could enjoy an illicit bourbon and the spectacular view of the city from the comfort of plush leather armchairs.

> **"THE PROGRAMME WAS SHORT ENOUGH – A FIXED BUDGET, no space more THAN TWENTY-EIGHT FEET FROM WINDOW TO CORRIDOR AND AS MANY STOREYS AS SUCH AS POSSIBLE ..."**

The stock market crash of 1929 did not affect the Chrysler Building as it was already well into the latter stages of construction. It could have devastated the construction of the third challenger for world's tallest building, though. Started a year later than the Chrysler Building, the Empire State Building was to become the archetypal skyscraper. Its architect Shreve, Lamb & Harmon created the landmark that still defines the American zeal and drive for life, wealth and greatness.

But this was no mere folly. The Empire State Building was a calculated economic gamble. William Lamb, chief designer, summed up the brief he was given: "The programme was short enough – a fixed budget, no space more than twenty-eight feet from window to corridor and as many storeys as such as possible. An exterior of limestone, and completion date of May first 1931, which meant a year and six months from the beginning of the sketches."

At its height construction on the Empire State Building raged around the clock. The prefabricated metal frame was raised at over a storey each day by a workforce of over 4000. Some 60,000 tonnes of steel, 10 million bricks and 200,000 tonnes of limestone and granite went into its construction. Seventy three lifts whisked staff at speeds of up to 427 metres per second from the ground-floor lobby to floors with, in total, twice as much lettable office space as the Chrysler Building. But perhaps the greatest achievement is that the building was completed $9 million under its estimated $50 million budget and many weeks early.

Without its antenna-like tip the Empire State Building was under a metre higher than the

Chrysler Building, at 320 metres. A 61-metre-high spire was added later, taking its height to 381 metres. The Empire State Building became the tallest of them all.

This colossus of a building had to recoup the investment put into it though and in the harsh financial climate of 1931 there were a distinct lack of companies ready to move into New York's newest status symbol. The Empire State Building became known as the "Empty State Building", as only one quarter of its floors were let. The Great Depression spelled lean times for Americans, but still construction went on in New York. The contract for the 29-storey, $42 million Waldorf Astoria hotel was signed on the day of the stock market crash, October 29, 1929.

Almost all of the huge block-wide footprint of the Waldorf Astoria is supported on steel pylons which span the tracks of the New York Central Railroad. The building was designed by architects Schultze & Weaver as a city under one roof. Its gargantuan bulk houses 2,200 rooms, ballrooms – including the largest one in the world at the time of construction – for 6,000 guests, bars, shops, kitchens and everything else that those rich enough to stay there could possibly want for.

Outwardly too, the building made a grand statement. Stark limestone wings gave way to a central tower of refined gothic lineage, which was topped by two patinated copper peaks, heavily detailed with triangular embossed designs and dragon-tail fins. The hotel was an art deco shrine to consumerism in a time of poverty in the United States, none the less it has survived and still plies its luxurious trade today.

However, as the 1930s progressed, the exquisitely detailed turrets and grand lobbies of the Waldorf, Chrysler et al began to lose their appeal. A new generation of architects was looking for a style with which to stamp their mark on New York. And, in 1936, the metropolis saw the dawning of a new architecture, one with less of a swagger but buckets full of style.

The name to stamp a more "modern" signature on the New York skyline was Rockefeller. Not with the famous Rockefeller Center, that would not be completed for another four years, but the Rockefeller apartments on 17 West 54th Street. Architects Harrison & Foulihoux made no attempt to drape the building in ornamentation, instead masonry walls are shaped to produce protruding semi-circular bays at the front of the apartments and minimal steel window frames almost slice apertures in the façade.

The Rockefellers went on to fund more significant architectural gestures in the years to come. In 1940 the completion of the Rockefeller Center signalled a new type of architecture.

Not a change in style, more an expansion of vision, the Rockefeller Center is an urban complex, a masterplan of buildings within one massive site on West 48th to West 51st Streets between Fifth and Sixth Avenues. A team of architects worked on the project between 1932–40. They included Raymond Hood; Corbett, Harrison & MacMurray; Godley & Foulihoux; and Reinhard & Hofmeister.

What these architects designed is a nod to the outgoing decorative era of art deco and a peek into the future of the Internationalist style. The Rockefeller Center was a private enterprise with commercially lettable space but it was also a home to the Metropolitan Opera. The Rockefellers commissioned grand artworks and even had an ice skating rink installed below ground.

The complex is as imposing today as it must have seemed in 1940. The huge central tower thrusts into the air, flanked by symmetrical towers and low-rise buildings in the same white and grey stone. This is architecture at its most imposing. Walk down Fifth Avenue and one can not help but be awed by the magnitude of the Rockefeller blocks standing strong and sublime above the noise of New York.

Ten years later, after a decade that included the Second World War, New York may not have noticed but the Rockefellers were building again. The Rockefeller Guest House is to the Rockefeller Center what chalk is to cheese. Sitting between two traditional stone and masonry town houses is architect Philip Johnson's ode to minimalism. The Guest House is Johnson indulging himself in his craft. This diminutive two-storey glass and masonry building is almost a flat roofed pavilion – private to the streetscape, with one door in a blank brick wall and beautifully open at the rear on to a formal sculpted garden. Philip Johnson has built many times in New York but this small apartment is exquisite, something by which he can always be judged.

Back in 1938 the New School for Social Research was opened on 66 West 12th Street. Joseph Urban's bold new statement took people by surprise. Its outward form leaned more towards a factory aesthetic. But inside, although devoid of trivial decoration, flowing curves dominate. From elliptical columns to illuminated, sculpted ceilings, the interior oozed class. The school's elliptical auditorium was Urban's *piece d' resistance*. Clad in perforated plaster panels and culminated in an arched stage set, it is understated and yet extremely beautiful.

In the late 1930s, while Europe was teetering on all out war and the Rockefellers were grappling with monumental architecture, the Museum of Modern Art (MoMA) decided it needed a new home. Founded in 1929, the museum collection had been housed in six rented rooms in the Crown Building. More space was required to be able to exhibit the entire collection and so Philip L. Goodwin and Edward Durrell Stone were commissioned and duly designed New York's first building in the International style.

Opened in 1939, the new MoMA building caused uproar. Its sleek façade of white marble and glass was seen as an affront to the traditional brownstone and flags of the street. Even though the museum was only seven storeys high and respected the existing building's setbacks it stuck out like a rather sleek sore thumb. And this would not be the last architectural debate to surround MoMA.

As MoMA's art collection grew so did its property portfolio. Philip Johnson first created the Grace Rainey Rogers Annex in 1951, and then the Abby Aldrich Rockefeller Sculpture Garden in 1953. In 1964 he designed an expansion with wings for photographic studies, drawings and prints and, in reverence of the building's initial creator, the Philip L Goodwin Galleries for architecture and design.

It was in 1977, when Cesar Pelli was asked to design a condominium tower and expansion on top of the original museum, that things got really ugly again. Critics of the project argued that the solution to MoMA's financial problem – rent out condos – was wrong on philosophical grounds. But dissent came loudest from groups opposed to the demolition of an adjacent Beaux-Arts town house; the intrusion of a tower in the middle of a side street; and the demolition of the original International Style façade. Eventually the façade was retained but the tower went up, completed in 1985.

Even as this book is being written MoMA is undergoing its latest transformation. The collection is currently exhibited over the East River in a disused factory in Queens, which has been converted by architects Cooper Robertson. Meanwhile major renovations and expansions are under way on the West 53rd Street site to a design by Yoshio Taniguchi. The new MoMA is set to reopen in 2005.

The years during and following the Second World War were lean times and no major development of note took place in New York. However, as the decade drew to a close, business was starting to get back to normal and companies were looking to build again. As in London, the war seemed to have swept out the last remnants of decorative architecture and a new clutch of talented designers influenced by the likes of Le Corbusier and the German Bauhaus school were coming to the fore. In fact, the Nazis are directly responsible for the rapid change in architectural style. They closed down the Bauhaus School, forcing teachers and pupils into exile. In the United States and Britain the architects put into practice their new modern, functional ideals.

One postwar building started a trend that has yet to be superseded. In 1947 a group of architects were picked from around the world to design the United Nations Secretariat building and General Assembly complex on First Avenue between 42nd and 48th Streets. Swiss architect Le Corbusier and Brazilian Oscar Niemeyer would stamp their mark on a team headed by American Wallace K. Harrison.

The design for a low slung General Assembly building and a 39-storey tower within a garden setting drew heavily on the aesthetic of the White City at the World Exposition of 1893 in Columbia and Le Corbusier's *Ville Radieuse*. But it was the glass curtain wall slab that adorned the tower's front and rear elevations that changed the direction of skyscraper architecture forever.

Le Corbusier, not the most team spirited architect, coveted the tower design for himself and produced the stunning 166 metre high block. However, his plan of natural ventilation using opening windows, protected by an awning of *brise soleil* was vetoed by lead architect Harrison. Instead, Harrison insisted upon air conditioning and designed the innovative curtain wall that sits 0.85 metres in front of the steel structure. This skin of blue-green heat-absorbing glass reflected in one tower a city soon to have many more.

From the UN Secretariat it was a short step to the great skyscrapers of the 1950s. In 1952 Lever House sprung up in double quick time thanks to curtain wall technology. Gordon Bunshaft's design for the "mini" skyscraper – it is only 21 storeys high – gave New Yorker's their first glimpse of an all-glass building. "Thin skin was in the air," said Bunshaft, the creative force behind Skidmore Owings & Merrill. Across the street from Lever House at 375 Park Avenue is the Seagram Building. Designed by Mies van der Rohe, this 38-storey tower clad in bronze glass and marble is seen as the ultimate in glass box architecture. Philip Johnson collaborated on the project which, when completed in 1958 at a cost of $41 million, was the most expensive building of its day.

Influenced by the public space at the foot of the Seagram Building, new zoning laws were introduced that required high rise buildings to provide some form of open space at their base. This has spawned many subsequent designs including skyscrapers on stilts (the Citicorp Center) and interior public gardens such as that at the 1967 Ford Foundation building by Roche/Dinkeloo & Associates Architects and Dan Kiley, landscape architect.

1959 saw the completion of one of the most recognizable buildings in the world, designed by one of the most talented American architects of any generation. Opened on October 21, 1959, the Solomon R. Guggenheim Museum is the creation of Frank Lloyd Wright. The museum had been designed some 15 years before but, delayed by the Second World War and the death of Solomon R. Guggenheim, it wasn't realized until the end of the 1950s.

Wright was a man surrounded by intrigue and controversy. His tumultuous private life had been fodder for society gossip columns for years and his outspoken belief in everything that he created ensured that he put numerous noses out of joint with this, his final project. Even before the ground had been broken on the site opposite the Metropolitan Museum, Wright exhorted: "Wait till you see the blueprints for the Guggenheim. It's going to make the Metropolitan look like a protestant barn."

For all his boasting the design was inspired. An upturned concrete spiral, creates a continuous ramp, up which people walk to view the artworks. Light pours in from a giant skylight, illuminating a central atrium to spectacular effect in this beautiful building. Externally Wright's creation is antithesis of everything surrounding it and in this it glorifies. But Wright blew the $750 000 budget for the project out of the water. The museum eventually cost nearly $2 million and the design was severely criticized by artists, who claimed that its curved walls were too small for the scale of their paintings. Wright brushed this aside, telling them to cut their paintings in half to fit his walls!

Wright never saw the completion of what many believe was his most brilliant creation. In the spring of 1959 he became ill and died on April 9. This brilliant, yet misunderstood, architect's legacy to New York is the instilling of a desire to create spaces of great beauty and ingenuity and he hasn't been let down. The Whitney Museum of American Art, by Marcel Breuer and Hamilton P Smith Architects, followed in 1966. Its upturned stepped pyramid

"WAIT TILL YOU **SEE THE BLUEPRINTS** FOR THE Guggenheim. IT'S GOING TO MAKE THE Metropolitan LOOK LIKE A **PROTESTANT BARN.**"

shape allowed for an open sculpture court at its centre, mimicking the Guggenheim's light-filled atrium in a modernist style. Breuer described the design as: "sculpture with rather serious functional requirements."

To this day museums are being built in New York. One of the newest is the American Folk Art Museum by Todd Williams and Billie Tsien. Opened in late 2001, next door to the site where MoMA is currently being rebuilt, this angular metal-panelled building looks almost impenetrable and foreboding from the exterior, while it is subtle and calm inside. The only windows on 53rd Street look out from the very corners of the building onto the Tishman Building and Eero Saarinen's monolithic block, the CBS Building.

Saarinen said of his design for the CBS Building: "I want to create the simplest skyscraper in New York." Unfortunately the architect did not live long enough to see the completion of the minimal masterpiece or his superb expressionist TWA Flight Center. He died in 1961 after completing the design for the CBS Building and while the TWA Flight Center was under construction.

"I WANT TO create THE **SIMPLEST** skyscraper IN NEW YORK."

In 1964, as the CBS Building was nearing completion, America became involved in the Vietnam War. The next eleven years were a physical and mental drain on America's resources and resolve. Building seemed of little relevance. Towers did still materialize – Bunshaft's Marine Midland Bank Building, 1967; General Motors Building by Edward Durrell Stone and Emery Roth & Sons, 1968; and the XYZ Buildings by Harrison, Abramovitz & Harris, for example – but one war stole the headlines of a decade.

Then, in 1975, as the Vietnam conflict came to an end, New Yorkers began to notice something major appearing on the skyline at the southern tip of Manhattan Island. Architect Minoru Yamasaki and US firm Emery Roth & Sons were building the World Trade Centers.

Yamasaki was a strange choice as lead architect of the World Trade Centers. He was not known for his tower designs, a 30-storey Detroit block being his largest to that date. And, he was extremely afraid of heights. His design surprised the architectural world too. Not a glass slab but two slender towers of great height, supported by external columns – a minimalist sculpture.

“IT SHOULD BE **UNIQUE**, HAVE AN EXCITEMENT OF ITS OWN, AND YET BE **RESPECTFUL** OF THE GENERAL AREA ... THAN BEING AN OVERPOWERING GROUP OF BUILDINGS, IT WILL BE **inviting, friendly and humane.**”

The best description of the towers, now scorched on a nation's memory, Is Yamasaki's letter to the design board, persuading them to go with his scheme. In it he writes: “In my opinion this should not be an overall form which melts into the multi-tiered landscape of Lower Manhattan. It should be unique, have an excitement of its own, and yet be respectful of the general area. The great scope of your project demands finding a way to scale it to a human being so that, rather than being an overpowering group of buildings, it will be inviting, friendly and humane.”

The 415 and 417 metre tall 110-storey twin towers plucked the mantle of “world's tallest” from the Empire State Building. Each floor boasted an acre of office space, thanks to Yamasaki's innovative external load-bearing skeleton. This was a truly iconic triumph of design and engineering and one that spawned at its feet a new financial quarter, including a gaggle of almost puny 34- to 51-storey towers – Cesar Pelli's Battery Park City (1985–92).

Throughout the early 1970s New York had been in decline but as investment in the city increased confidence returned and the towers kept on coming. In 1976 and later 1983 the angled glass blocks of One and Two UN Plaza rose opposite the UN Secretariat. In 1984 Philip Johnson and John Burgee's post modern AT&T Building came to fruition and 1986 saw Johnson's beautifully curved, “telescopic” Lipstick building up the ante in fashionable skyscraper design.

During this time one skyscraper broke new ground in its innovation. In 1978 the Citicorp Center was completed on Lexington Avenue between East 53rd and 54th Streets. Built on four gigantic columns, set at the middle of each elevation rather than the corners, the Citicorp Center was the first skyscraper to incorporate a mass tombed damper system. High up, some

270 metres, in the building's sloping peak, a huge block of concrete sits on a bed of oil. When this extremely high super-light skyscraper sways in the wind its movements are monitored on computer and the concrete block is set in motion on its pad of oil. By transferring its inertia to the building structure the block reduces the building's motion by half.

However, poor construction techniques can come home to haunt even the best architect and Hugh Stubbins found after completion that joints in Citicorp's diagonal windbraces that should have been welded were actually bolted together. It was calculated that winds strong enough to shear these bolts could occur around once every 16 years in New York and so welders had to work around the clock securing steel reinforcing plates over the joints of every diagonal windbrace on the massive building.

As the booming 1980s drew to a close commercial space was becoming rare in New York and since then only a handful of large towers have been built. Three of the best examples are the Carnegie Hall Tower by Pelli (1991); Four Times Square by Fox & Fowle (1999); and the LVMH by Atelier Christian de Portzamparc (2000).

Architects it seemed would have to find a different way of expressing themselves in the Big Apple. And so they did, or rather it seems European architects did. Retail has become the place to be in the new millennium. As high fashion revels in its status as the new rock and roll, fashion design houses are employing world-renowned architects to fit out their flagship stores. Helmut Lang employed Gluckman Mayner Architects to radically redesign its Greene Street store – it got an art gallery. Minimal white walls and a concrete floor are home to four large boxes that hide clothes from window shoppers.

UK practice Future Systems' created stores for Marni and Commes des Garçons in SoHo. And now Issey Miyake and Prada are battling for supremacy, employing two of the biggest names in architecture today – Frank Gehry and Rem Koolhaas respectively – to do a bit of interior decorating. Both architects use trademark styles on their shop projects. Gehry, in collaboration with local architect G-Tech, has converted a two-storey Tribecca store into a metal sculpture. Thin curved steel sheet twists and slices its way from the checkout, over customer's heads and down into the basement level of the store. It is a triumph of sculptural form, complimenting the designs of Issey Miyake perfectly.

Koolhaas meanwhile, has forged ahead with high-tech materials and quirky ideas in the much larger Broadway store. A wooden floor swoops from ground-floor level into the basement and back up again. A circular glass lift ferries shoppers between floors and the changing rooms are constructed of glass that changes from clear to translucent when they are occupied.

This trend for architecturally inspired interiors is merely a hiatus in the city's quest for further architectural glory. New York has yet to give up on finding room for landmark structures. In a sliver of a site on 52nd Street, between two much wider buildings Austrian architect Raimund Abraham has just put the finishing touches to the new Austrian Cultural Forum. The 24-storey building has only one visible elevation, a raked façade of zinc and glass. Out of this slice of the future protrudes glass fronted zinc box. The design is a triumph of the abstract and intriguing, futuristic without being comic book pastiche.

And so to the future. Italian architect Renzo Piano has started work on the refurbishment and extension of the Pierpont Morgan Gallery and US practice Diller + Scofidio has won the competition to design a $60 million media institute for Eyebeam, the New York arts organization dedicated to new media artworks. The practice's proposal of a 12-storey building made of a two-ply ribbon-like system of fibreglass and concrete that has two contrasting faces will see yet another architectural innovation unleashed on to the city. The project is due for completion in 2007.

As New York forges its way into the twenty-first century, one project is at the forefront of all city dwellers' minds. What will be built on the site of the World Trade Centers? The man assigned with the task of finding a vision for Ground Zero is Alex Garvin. As vice president for planning, design and development at the Lower Manhattan Development Corporation Garvin has a tough task ahead of him. Perhaps he should revisit Yamasaki's initial letter about the World Trade Centers' design for inspiration: "...it should be unique, have an excitement of its own and yet be respectful to the general area...rather than being overpowering it will be inviting, friendly and humane." If Garvin can capture the essence of Yamasaki's words he will create a fitting tribute to those who died on September 11, 2001.

ARK

GRAND CENTRAL
TERMINAL

THE WALDORF-ASTORIA

MoMA
The Museum of Modern Art
MoMA
The Museum of Modern Art
MASTERWORKS

SOLOMON R GUGGENHEIM MUSEUM

GUGGENHEIM

Gates 21 thru 32

MADISON AV

Thank you for riding the Long Island Rail Road

BUFFALO
DAVID BITTON
TDK
OSHKOSH
WHAT THE FUTURE WEARS.
LG

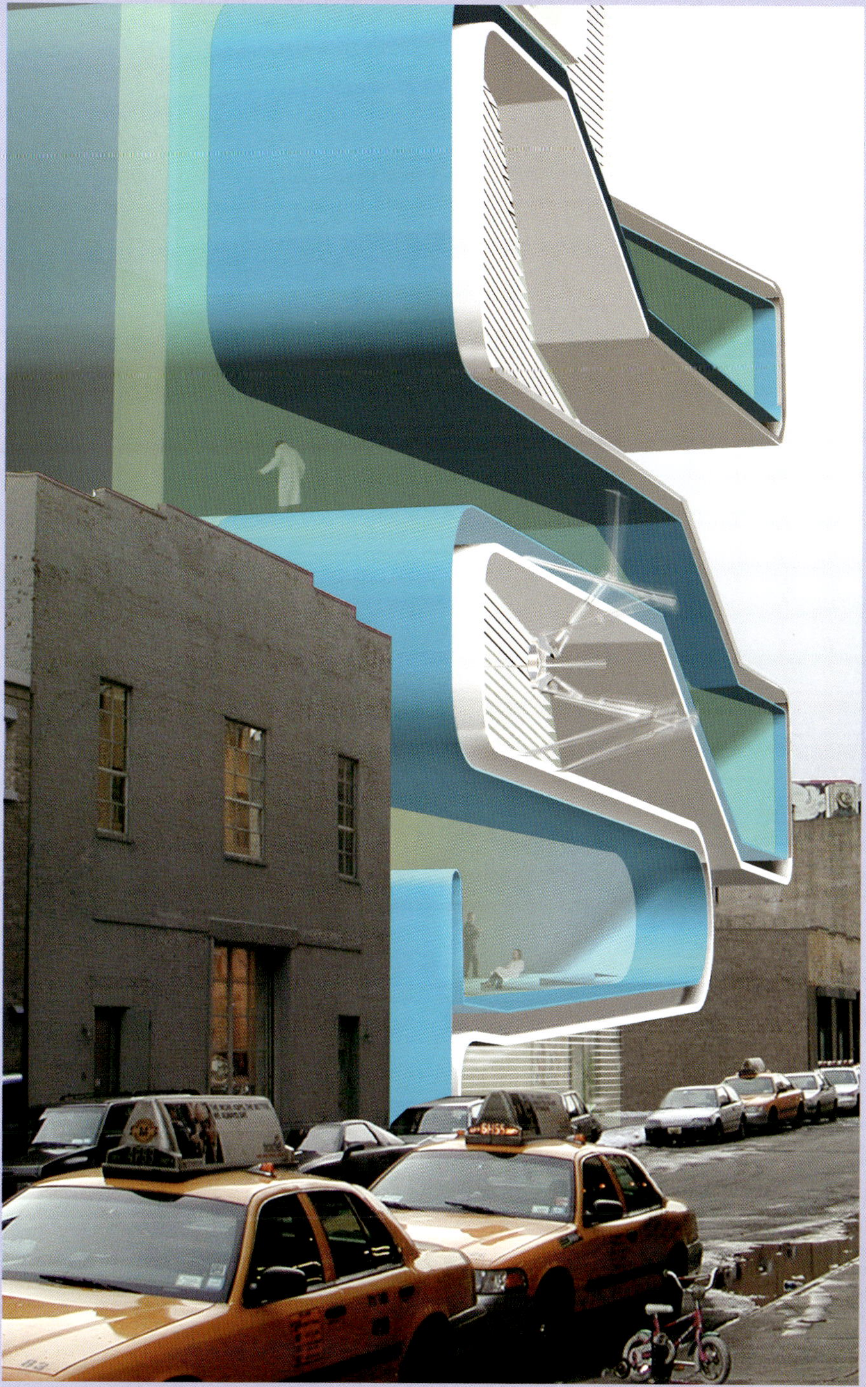

BROOKLYN BRIDGE

Designed and built by engineer John Augustus Roebling and, after his death, his son Washington. The bridge took 24 years to build and was completed in 1883.

OLD MANHATTAN

The city pushed skyward from the turn of the century. This picture shows the southern tip of Manhattan Island in the 1920s.

EMPIRE STATE BUILDING/BATTERY PARK

The Empire State Building (left) possibly the greatest architectural achievement of the 1930s. Cesar Pelli's Battery Park City buildings (right) were dwarfed by the World Trade Centers,

CHRYSLER BUILDING

Plush wall panelling and beautiful decorative glazing signal the Art Deco period, here in William van Alen's Chrysler Building.

TIMES SQUARE

In all its neon glory Times Square is the hub of New York's theatreland and a mecca for tourists. City officials actively encourage illuminated signage on the area's buildings.

CENTRAL PARK

For all the city's defining architectural statements, one of the most awe-inspiring sites is the vast green space of Central Park, designed by Frederick Law Olmsted and Calvert Vaux, the park was constructed between 1859 and 1876.

BROOKLYN BRIDGE

Roebling's engineering masterpiece, the Brooklyn Bridge spans 486 metres and stands 84 metres above the high water line. Roebling died while building the bridge.

FULLER BUILDING

The Fuller Building, also known as the Flat Iron due to its shape, was designed by Daniel Burnham and completed in 1903. It is one of the finest examples of cast iron architecture, and its façade features exquisite detailing on the upper floors.

SINGER BUILDING/WOOLWORTH BUILDING

Ernest Flagg's 1904 Singer Building (left) showed the true merits of building with iron – high rise architecture with large window apertures. Cass Gilbert's 1913 Woolworth Building (right) became the world's tallest building at 241 metres.

GRAND CENTRAL STATION

Designed by Warren & Wetmore, Reed and Stem Architects Grand Central Station was completed in 1913. Its cathedral-like ticket hall is still beautifully spacious and calming, even during rush hour.

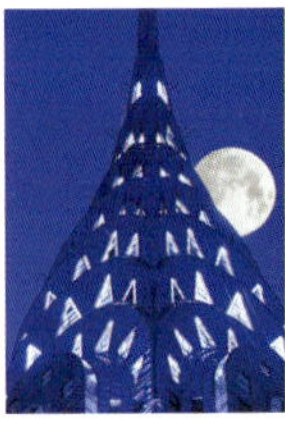

CHRYSLER BUILDING/EMPIRE STATE BUILDING

The chrome covered tip of New York's most beautiful skyscraper, the Chrysler Building, designed by William van Alen. It's chrome vertex pushes it to 319.5 metres tall, but it is dwarfed by the Empire State Building which peaks at 381 metres.

EMPIRE STATE/WALDORF ASTORIA HOTEL

Shreve, Lamb and Harmon designed New York's most famous architectural feat, the Empire State Building. It's viewing deck is the most visited tourist attraction in the city. The Waldorf Astoria (right) is the epitome of luxury and wealth both inside and out.

NEW SCHOOL FOR SOCIAL RESEARCH

Joseph Urban's New School For Social Research was opened in 1938. It featured a beautifully conceived elliptical auditorium. The walls and ceiling are clad in perforated plastered to enhance the acoustics.

ROCKEFELLER APARTMENTS AND CENTER

Harrison and Foulihoux's Rockefeller Apartments of 1936 (left) heralded the dawning of the modern movement. The Rockefeller Center's austere, imposing bulk (right) hides a skating ring at its heart.

MUSEUM OF MODERN ART

MoMA opened to public outcry in 1939. Philip L. Goodwin and Edward Durrell Stone's museum in the International Style incited debate in architectural and public circles. MoMA's interior (right) looking out on to the sculpture garden.

UNITED NATIONS BUILDING/LEVER HOUSE

Beautifully simple aesthetically, Le Corbusier's 1947 UN Secretariat (left) featured the first glass curtain wall in New York. Lever House (right) designed by Gordon Bunshaft and completed in 1952 was the city's first all-glass building.

SEAGRAM BUILDING

Mies van der Rohe's Seagram Building cost $41 million in 1958, It is still considered one of the finest examples of glass box architecture. The façade detail (right) shows great attention to proportion and form.

SOLOMON R. GUGGENHEIM MUSEUM

Frank Lloyd Wright died in 1959, only months before the opening of his most famous work, the Solomon R. Guggenheim Musuem.

TWA FLIGHT CENTER

The TWA Flight Center at JFK Airport is one of the most beautiful concrete buildings ever built. It was designed by Eero Saarinen.

TWA FLIGHT CENTER – INTERIOR

Saarinen's TWA flight center is as sculpturally beautiful inside as it looks from the exterior – the architect died while the building was being constructed.

CHASE MANHATTAN/CBS/LINCOLN CENTER

Skidmore, Owings & Merrill's Chase Manhattan Plaza (left, top) and Eero Saarinen's CBS building (left, bottom). Architects on the Lincoln Center (right), constructed in the 1960s, included Philip Johnson, Eero Saarinen, Pietro Belluschi and SOM. The master plan was by Wallace K Harrison.

FORD FOUNDATION/WHITNEY MUSEUM

The Ford Foundation (left) by Roche-Dinkeloo, features a huge glazed atrium with a large indoor garden area. Marcel Breuer's Whitney Museum of American Art (right) is an upturned, stepped pyramid with an open sculpture court at its centre.

WORLD TRADE CENTERS

Minoru Yamasaki created the ultimate in architectural sculpture with his minimal but massive World Trade Centers. Here they are seen as they were from beneath Brooklyn Bridge.

CITICORP CENTER/SONY PLAZA

The Citicorp Center (left) is a skyscraper on stilts, it was the first building to feature a mass damping system to stop it swaying in high winds. Philip Johnson's AT&T Building (right) is now the Sony Plaza.

JACOB K. JAVITS CENTER/LIPSTICK BUILDING

Looking out from I.M. Pei & Partners Jacob J. Javits Convention Center towards the Empire State Building. Philip Johnson's stylish elliptical 886 Third Avenue is known as the Lipstick Building for its likeness to expensive cosmetics packaging.

NOBU/LONG ISLAND RAILROAD

Nobu (left), the most stylish of sushi houses, was designed by the Rockwell Group in 1994 for owner Robert De Niro. A striking tower of steel and glass signals the entrance to the Long Island Rail Road (right), designed by RM Kliment & Frances Halsband.

FOUR TIMES SQUARE/501 WEST 23RD STREET

Fox & Fowle's Four Times Square (left, 1999) refers to numerous architectural styles to create one of its own. Designed by Smith Thompson Associates 501 West 23rd Street (right, 1999) functions as a living space and work studio for its designers.

AMERICAN FOLK ART MUSEUM/ROSE CENTER

The American Folk Art Museum (left) by Todd Wiliams and Billie Tsien opened in 2001 next to the site on which MoMA is being re-built. The Rose Center for Earth and Space (right, 2000) is the Polshek Partnership's triumph in h-itech architecture.

NEW YORK STYLE

Clockwise from top left: Prada (2001) by Rem Koolhaas and OMA; Helmut Lang (1997) by Gluckman Mayer Architects; Issey Miyake (2001) by Frank Gehry and G-Tech and the interior of the LVMH Tower, designed by Atelier Christian de Portzamparc in 2000.

AUSTRIAN CULTURAL FORUM/EYEBEAM

The Austrian Cultural Forum (left) is a raking sliver of metal and glass designed by Raimund Abraham. Architect Diller & Scofidio's futuristic plans for a media institute for Eyebeam (right), the New York arts organization dedicated to new media artworks.

Picture credits

The publishers would like to thank the following sources for their kind permission to reproduce the pictures in this book:

Arcaid: Alex Bartel 8/9, 62 / David Churchill 57 3350/10/1 / Mark Fiennes 42, 45 /Neil Troiano 66 / Richard Waite 5 Corbis :2/3, 33 /Paul Almasy 44/Robert Holmes 56Angelo Hornak 46, 54 top left, 54 top right, 60/ /Thomas A. Kelly 37 bottom, 64 / G.E. Kidders Smith 54 bottom right, 54 bottom left / Bob Krist 69 / Gail Mooney 43 / Vince Streano 26/27Michael S. Yamashita 55 Diller & Scofidio: 73 Getty Images: Alain Choisnet 4 / Grant V. Faint 34 / Michele-Salmieri 35 Marvin E. Newman 41 / James Porto 36 / Bruce Stoddard 24/25, / Margaret Stratton 28 (c) The Solomon R. Guggenheim Foundation, New York: David Heald 48, 49 R.M. Kliment & Frances Halsband Architects: Cervin Robinson 6 Norman McGrath: 7, 61, 63, Michael Moran: 29, 30, 31, 32, 38/39, 40, 47, 50/51, 68, 70 top, 72.Smith and Thompson Architects: 67Topham Picturepoint: ImageWorks 37 top View: Nathan Wilcock 1, 52/53, 58/59 Paul Warchol: 70 bottom, 71 bottom, 71 top.

Every effort has been made to acknowledge correctly and contact the source and/or copyright holder of each picture, and Carlton Books Limited apologises for any unintentional errors or omissions which will be corrected in future editions of this book.